Security Delivery Platforms

FOR DUMMIES®

A Wiley Brand

Gigamon Special Edition

by Crystal Bedell and
Steve Piper, CISSP

FOR DUMMIES®

A Wiley Brand

Security Delivery Platforms For Dummies®, Gigamon Special Edition

Published by
John Wiley & Sons, Inc.
111 River St.
Hoboken, NJ 07030-5774
www.wiley.com

For general information on our other products and services, or how to create a custom *For Dummies* book for your business or organization, please contact our Business Development Department in the U.S. at 877-409-4177, contact info@dummies.biz, or visit www.wiley.com/go/custompub. For information about licensing the *For Dummies* brand for products or services, contact BrandedRights&Licenses@Wiley.com.

ISBN: 978-1-119-25907-7 (pbk); ISBN: 978-1-119-25910-7 (ebk)

Manufactured in the United States of America

10 9 8 7 6 5 4 3 2 1

Publisher's Acknowledgments

Some of the people who helped bring this book to market include the following:

Project Editor: Carrie A. Burchfield

Development Editor: Kathy Simpson

Acquisitions Editor: Amy Fandrei

Editorial Manager: Rev Mengle

Business Development Representative: Karen Hattan

Production Editor: Kumar Chellappan

Special Help from Gigamon: Shannon Albert, Jai Balasubramaniyan, Liz Garcia, Johnnie Konstantas, Tony Nguyen, Erin O'Malley, Ananda Rajagopal, Patrick Riley, Sesh Sayani

Table of Contents

Introduction

● ●

Despite a plethora of network security and monitoring tools, detecting and responding to cyberthreats are increasingly challenging tasks. The very nature of corporate networks and the way in which security tools are deployed put IT teams at a clear disadvantage.

The corporate network is no longer a static, well-defined entity that can be adequately protected with an armory of perimeter-based security tools. Instead, it's an amorphous, dynamic entity that extends well beyond the four walls of the data center. Technologies such as cloud computing, virtualization, and mobile computing add to the complexity.

Meanwhile, IT teams must shoehorn security tools into the network infrastructure and hope that their limited view of traffic will be enough to expose the low-and-slow activity that's characteristic of advanced threats. But as long as there are blind spots on the network, there's a chance that malicious activity is going undetected.

IT organizations need a new approach that enables visibility across the entire IT infrastructure, including physical, virtual, and cloud environments. They need a security delivery platform.

About This Book

This book introduces IT professionals to security delivery platforms, a class of technology that transforms how security and monitoring tools are deployed on the network to provide pervasive visibility. But security delivery platforms don't just deliver traffic to security tools. They also offload intensive traffic-inspection processes and deliver the right traffic to the right tool, helping you optimize your security tools for greater efficacy and increased return on investment.

If you're responsible for protecting a corporate network or managing the deployment of security tools, this book is for you.

Foolish Assumptions

In preparing this book, we assumed a few things about you, the reader:

- ✔ You work in the IT security field for a corporation, government agency, or services firm.
- ✔ You have foundational knowledge of computers, computer networking, and network security concepts, but you're not necessarily familiar with network test access points (TAPs) or network visibility.
- ✔ You're familiar with common network interfaces, including 10/100/1000 copper, 1 Gbps fiber, and 10 Gbps fiber.

Icons Used in This Book

This book uses the following icons to indicate special content.

You won't want to forget the information in these paragraphs.

A Tip icon points out practical advice that can help you craft a better strategy, whether you're planning a purchase or setting up your software.

Look out! When you see this icon, it's time to pay attention. You won't want to miss this cautionary information.

Maybe you're one of those highly detailed people who really need to grasp all the nuts and bolts — even the most techie parts. If so, these tidbits are right up your alley.

Beyond the Book

This book explores security delivery platforms in great detail, but if you crave more, we encourage you to visit `https://www.gigamon.com`.

Chapter 1

Addressing the New Threat Landscape

*L*et's face it: Hacking and cyberthreats have come a long way since the mid-1990s. Hackers are no longer lone wolves writing crude viruses in their parents' basements. Their goal is no longer to take advantage of any opportunity to disrupt services or show off their skills. They've gotten much more sophisticated, and so have their attacks.

This chapter discusses modern cyberthreats and common defenses used against them.

Surveying the Modern Security Landscape

Today, cybercriminals work together to evolve their techniques and trade intellectual property. Typically, they are well-funded nation–states or organized cybercriminals, and they have specific targets in mind. Often, the goal is to exfiltrate valuable data that can be sold on the black market or used to blackmail the victims.

Threats have evolved from quick-and-dirty viruses that leave destruction in their wake to complex, low-and-slow attacks that bypass signature-based tools. These advanced persistent threats (APTs) employ sophisticated methods to compromise the network and persist for long periods without being detected by network operators.

While cybercriminals have evolved their tactics, the methods for protecting corporate networks have stayed relatively unchanged.

Reviewing common network defenses

Traditional security defense strategies, which many companies continue to use, are based on three simple assumptions:

- **A perimeter around the network can keep the bad guys out and the good guys in.** Perimeter security defenses typically include a firewall at the Internet edge and endpoint security software, such as an antivirus tool, on client devices.

- **The network perimeter is static.** Security appliances such as firewalls, intrusion detection/prevention systems, and other malware detection systems are deployed at fixed locations along the network perimeter where traffic is expected to travel. Traffic is monitored as it passes through these choke points.

- **Employees are to be trusted, and everyone else is not to be trusted.** This simple trust model extends to the devices on the network. In this model, the devices are IT-owned and managed, with the right build of software, patches, and antivirus protection, so they can be trusted.

Several IT trends are breaking these assumptions, however, as you will see in the next section.

Identifying IT trends that affect security

The following trends are having significant effects on most organizations' security practices:

✔ **Consumerization of IT:** Thanks to the consumerization of IT and "bring your own device" (BYOD) policies, employees expect to be able to access corporate data and network resources from personally owned devices. As a result, IT has had little choice but to loosen the strict controls on computers, laptops, smartphones, and other mobile devices, making all of them vulnerable to malware infection.

✔ **New technologies:** Innovations in enterprise IT are driving business-model change as organizations use technology for competitive and operational advantages. Even as they uncover new lines of revenue and improve internal efficiencies, these technologies fly in the face of IT assumptions about the environment.

Consider, for example, server virtualization and multitier application design. Both technologies drive a shift in data center traffic patterns compared to traditional monolithic client-server applications. Instead of network traffic only moving north/south from the client to the server and back, the majority of network traffic flows east/west between virtual machines (VMs) and application servers and databases. As a result, security appliances concentrated at the network egress and ingress points never see this traffic.

✔ **Tool complexity:** All these trends are compounded by the complexity and fragmentation of legacy security tools. Most organizations have dozens of security technologies that don't interoperate.

✔ **Lack of security talent:** The problem of tool complexity is exacerbated by a significant lack of security talent available in the market. Too few security professionals available for hire understand how to manage the various technologies.

Seeing the Limitations of Existing Security Deployments

Many of today's security architectures include important detection, prevention, and analytics tools that use network traffic to perform their functions. A typical legacy deployment directly connects such tools to the network through a switch port analyzer (SPAN) or mirror port on a network switch/router. Some deployments connect such security tools directly to a network test access point (TAP).

In this section, we describe a few of the challenges of working with legacy security deployment.

Active versus passive tools

As a network expands, providing access to a multitude of passive and active security tools becomes more difficult. Most modern networks have defense-in-depth security architectures comprised of dozens of active and passive security tools — a situation that presents numerous challenges.

Active (or *inline*) *tools* sit in the direct path of traffic and can block, allow, or modify packets as they move across the network. Active tools typically perform some form of protection or prevention function. Examples of active tools include the following:

- ✔ Intrusion prevention system (IPS)

- ✔ Next-generation firewall (NGFW)

- ✔ Distributed denial of service (DDoS) prevention

- ✔ Web application firewall (WAF)

- ✔ Data-loss prevention (DLP) system

Passive (or *out-of-band*) *tools* sit outside the direct path of traffic to inspect that traffic. They use both TAP and SPAN or mirror ports to connect to the network. Passive tools are typically deployed to perform anomaly detection or other analysis without affecting the production network. Following are a few examples of passive tools:

- ✔ Intrusion detection systems (IDS)

- ✔ Advanced malware detection systems

- ✔ Network behavior analysis solutions

- ✔ Network forensics tools

Lack of network access points

Directly connecting a security tool to a network TAP (see Chapter 2) or a SPAN port (see the nearby sidebar) allows that tool to see the traffic on that portion of the network. The problem is that organizations typically have far more monitoring and security tools than they do network access points.

Network operations roadblocks

As you can imagine — and may have experienced yourself — when SPAN-port contention (see the nearby sidebar) meets appliance sprawl, a dark cloud descends over IT. SPAN-port contention and appliance sprawl commonly pit network operations against security operations. Security ops wants every tool to have full visibility of the network, and network ops is charged with hunting down an open SPAN port for each tool.

The problem with SPAN ports

When organizations have more passive security tools than they have switch SPAN ports by which to connect them to the network, the result is *SPAN-port contention*. This problem is a common one, given that most network switches have only a limited number of SPAN ports (usually two).

The implications of SPAN-port contention aren't pretty. Security operations isn't the only group that wants access to SPAN ports; IT and network operations also have network devices that they want to connect to these interfaces. With all three groups vying for access to network traffic — for legitimate reasons — who gets to connect?

The truth is that SPAN ports shouldn't be used to access traffic for passive security analysis. The technology wasn't built for reliable long-term security monitoring. SPAN ports are known to drop packets, misorder packets, stop forwarding packets when the switch is busy with a higher-priority task, and become intermittently or chronically oversubscribed (and then drop even more packets). At 10 Gbps speeds and above, the full bandwidth of the monitor port may not even be available. Also, as use of the SPAN port rises above 7 Gbps, production network packets may be dropped to monitor port packets.

Yet another point of dissension involves tool failure. Active security appliances sit inline so that they can block malicious traffic. But if a security tool fails, business-critical traffic and communications are interrupted, which can adversely affect revenue — and satisfaction with the network ops team. Consequently, upgrading active security tools that sit inline often requires complex coordination between network ops and security ops teams to find a suitable maintenance window.

For details on solving these challenges, see Chapter 4.

Limited network visibility

You can't protect what you can't see. Security appliances connected to specific points of the network may not see traffic from other parts of the network, which results in blind spots with respect to security coverage.

Furthermore, as we mention in "Identifying IT trends that affect security" earlier in this chapter, traffic that flows east/west inside data centers (particularly traffic contained in virtualized network segments) often doesn't have the benefit of security inspection. This situation exacerbates the security blind-spot problem, making security less effective.

We discuss how to solve this problem in Chapter 5.

SSL-encrypted blind spots

More and more applications use SSL (Secure Sockets Layer) encryption to protect data in motion. By rendering traffic unreadable by attackers, however, these applications also render traffic unreadable by legitimate monitoring tools. Attackers know this situation and use encryption themselves to hide their activities. Some monitoring tools decrypt SSL traffic — for a price. Both network performance and your budget take a hit because decryption functionality adds to your licensing costs.

Find out how to solve this problem in Chapter 8.

Chapter 2

Understanding Security Delivery Platforms

*T*he security industry is by no means standing still in its fight against cyberthreats. Technology providers and security researchers are continually evolving their security efforts.

These efforts, however, focus on the growing sophistication of the security tools themselves. Little attention is being paid to the deployment architecture for these tools, which leads to many of the challenges we describe in Chapter 1.

Clearly, it's time to rethink how security tools are deployed on the network. Organizations need an approach that takes the guesswork out of where to deploy security tools and eliminates dependence on static choke points.

In this chapter, we introduce that approach: a security delivery platform.

What Is a Security Delivery Platform?

A *security delivery platform* (SDP), as depicted in Figure 2-1, is a structured, platform-based approach to providing traffic visibility to a variety of security tools concurrently. An SDP is designed to do so in a scalable, pervasive, and cost-effective manner.

Figure 2-1: An SDP provides traffic visibility to multiple security tools concurrently.

By providing pervasive visibility across the entire network, an SDP can help advanced threat detection systems more accurately spot bad actors and malware as they move across the network; reduce the time to detection of suspicious activity; and significantly reduce the typical overhead, complexity, and cost of deploying security tools.

An SDP consists of several components, which we discuss in the sections that follow.

Network TAPs

A *network test access point* (TAP) is a simple hardware device that connects to the cabling infrastructure used to connect two network devices. Check out Figure 2-2. The network TAP copies packets and sends them to passive (out-of-band) security monitoring tools.

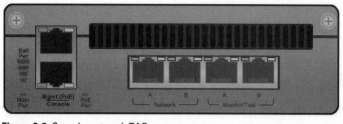

Figure 2-2: Sample network TAP.

Using network TAPs is the most effective way to direct network traffic from a single source to one or more passive security tools. TAPs are available for a wide variety of network speeds and cable types.

A network TAP doesn't insert traffic from the connected tool back into the network, so it can't be used to deliver traffic to an active security tool. A special type of TAP, called a *bypass TAP*, is used to place a security tool inline.

Network visibility appliances

Think of the network visibility appliances as a web of intelligent traffic-manipulation devices. Unlike TAPs, which are primarily used to send copies of traffic to passive security tools, network visibility appliances support both active and passive deployments. (We cover this more in the upcoming section "How a Network Visibility Appliance Works.")

A network visibility appliance is designed to help network security and network performance tools run more efficiently. It enables security tools to get applicable traffic feeds from across the infrastructure in a cost-effective, scale-out manner. That's not all, though. The appliance also acts on those traffic streams and performs a variety of functions that can be offloaded from the security tools to optimize their performance.

A typical appliance is rack mounted with copper and/or fiber interfaces. It takes network traffic from TAPs or switch SPAN ports, or it sits inline between two connected routers or switches. The appliance filters or manipulates traffic before passing it to the appropriate network security or performance tool. These actions (such as packet masking, de-duplication, and header stripping) help address security, performance, and privacy concerns.

Network visibility appliances are the heart of any SDP deployment, so much of this book refers to their role. Network visibility appliances provide many-to-many port mapping of network ports to monitoring ports, as well as the following basic features:

- ✔ Configuration interface
- ✔ Packet filtering, slicing, and de-duplication
- ✔ Traffic aggregation, regeneration, and load balancing

Virtual network visibility appliances

Network visibility appliances are also available as virtualized nodes, which give visibility to traffic associated with virtualized workloads. Virtual appliances can track virtual machines (VMs) as they move from host to host. "Follow the VM" policies ensure that application traffic is always sent to the security tools even as the VMs move.

Application programming interface (API)

Network visibility appliances can also include an *application programming interface* (API) — a set of programming instructions that specifies how software components interact.

An API allows security tools to adjust, in near real time, the traffic feeds that they receive from an appliance. If a security tool detects anomalies, threats, or other predefined conditions in the traffic streams it's receiving, the tool can modify its visibility into the network by controlling the traffic feeds it receives from the network visibility appliance. This modification is automated via an API.

Management console

IT needs a way to access and control the components of the SDP. This is done via a centralized management console. The console enables IT to centrally manage traffic distribution for physical and virtual network visibility appliances and also exposes the APIs.

How a Network Visibility Appliance Works

A network visibility appliance connects to the network across physical and virtual infrastructures to deliver the right traffic to the right security tool. Security tools simply connect to the appliance to receive relevant traffic streams from across the network infrastructure.

A network visibility appliance offers several capabilities, which we discuss in the following sections.

Supporting active and passive deployments

A network visibility appliance can support a variety of active and passive security tools in parallel, as shown in Figure 2-3.

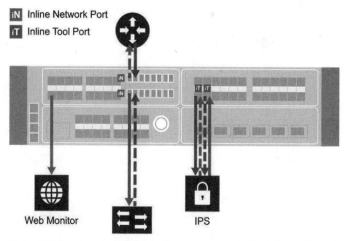

Figure 2-3: A network visibility appliance supports both active and passive tools.

Active (or inline) security tools can act on traffic when they detect threats, malware, or anomalous behavior. In supporting these tools, the appliance provides full failure protection to achieve fault tolerance. To avoid overloading any single tool, it can perform traffic distribution.

The network visibility appliance also accommodates deployment of passive security tools, which monitor traffic for malware or suspicious activity and which can perform forensics after a security incident occurs.

Aggregating traffic

A network visibility appliance provides a cost-effective way to achieve full traffic visibility without unnecessarily deploying additional security tools across the network. It collects traffic from multiple sources, eliminating potential blind spots.

A network visibility appliance also provides visibility into east/west traffic, as well as traffic traversing the internal campus and data-center networks. By addressing VM mobility problems, the visibility appliance can provide a consistent source of traffic to security tools, enabling them to identify threats that attempt to move laterally across the network and to expose the actions of bad actors.

Regenerating traffic for multiple security tools

Sometimes, multiple security tools need to inspect the same traffic streams. A network visibility appliance can copy relevant traffic streams and deliver them to the appropriate security tools. Because contention for traffic isn't a problem, IT organizations no longer have to decide which tool to use at any given time; instead, they can use all their security tools at all times.

Network Visibility Appliance Benefits

A network visibility appliance offers several benefits, which we discuss in the following sections.

Aggregating dispersed physical and virtual traffic

Collecting physical and virtual traffic flowing among physical and virtualized workloads provides security tools full visibility into users, devices, and applications regardless of where they're located. IT no longer has to worry, for example, when a VM moves to a different host or even data center. Network blind spots become things of the past, as the appliance provides every security tool consistent visibility into traffic across distributed networks.

Extending the life of network security tools

Given the increase in network traffic, more IT organizations are migrating to 10 Gbps (or even 40 Gbps/100 Gbps) networks. Unfortunately, in a traditional deployment scenario, this migration renders existing 1 Gbps monitoring tools useless because they can't process at 10 Gbps speed. Figure 2-4 illustrates how a network visibility appliance solves this problem.

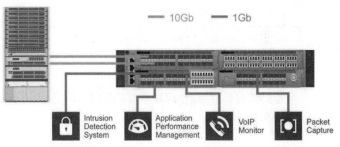

Figure 2-4: Network visibility appliances extend the life of 1 Gbps monitoring tools.

Because a network visibility appliance can bridge between speeds and can divide traffic across multiple tools, you can continue to use 1 Gbps network and security tools — as long as the destined traffic volume doesn't exceed the 1 Gbps tool's processing capacity.

Optimizing existing infrastructure

The performance of the existing infrastructure can be optimized by offloading resource-intensive tasks from network and security devices. By taking on additional functions, such as NetFlow generation (see Chapter 6) and SSL decryption (see Chapter 8), the network visibility appliance enables IT to leverage these capabilities across the entire IT environment while freeing resources for more effective, efficient inspection of traffic.

Decrypting SSL traffic

As we mention in Chapter 1, SSL encryption helps bad actors hide their activities just as effectively as it helps organizations protect their private or sensitive data. As the number and types of attacks that leverage encrypted communications increase, so does the need to inspect SSL-encrypted traffic.

A network visibility appliance can decrypt SSL traffic, thereby eliminating this blind spot for security tools. Some security tools have the ability to decrypt SSL traffic, but decryption is a computationally intensive task that must be performed by every tool that requires it. Offloading SSL decryption to the appliance helps these security tools run more efficiently. In addition to returning security tools to full performance, offloading SSL decryption eliminates the need to install SSL certificates and keys on multiple tools, thereby reducing administration costs.

Extracting application sessions of interest

When you think about the volume of traffic that security and monitoring tools must inspect to identify threats, you can begin to appreciate the enormity of this task. Every packet must be analyzed for its materiality to a network attack. This analysis is performed using, in many cases, multiple techniques and security devices. Some of these security appliances, such as email security gateways and web application firewalls, are specialized to inspect only certain applications or protocols. They must expend precious CPU cycles filtering out the traffic that they consider to be irrelevant, which has a negative effect on security efficacy.

A network visibility appliance that provides application session filtering (see Figure 2-5) can make security tools more efficient by forwarding specific streams of traffic to them. The visibility appliance looks at the application layer of a packet and identifies application flows. Then it directs entire sessions to the appropriate security tool, including those packets that are part of the session setup, so that the security tool can see all the context for the flow. With application session filtering, the IT organization can designate what constitutes a relevant traffic stream for each security tool and set up forwarding rules so that traffic is delivered accordingly.

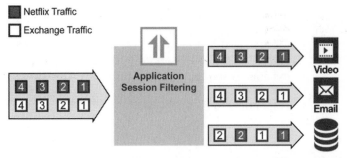

Figure 2-5: Application session filtering in a network visibility appliance.

Extending visibility

Security tools are only as effective as the network traffic they're configured to see, and this visibility is rapidly dwindling. Blind spots are proliferating across networks thanks to the growing complexity of networks. This complexity comes from the broadening adoption of virtualized workloads and services, as well as a dissolving network perimeter thanks to the proliferation of bring your own device (BYOD) policies and mobility.

Network visibility appliances provide pervasive visibility across the entire IT environment by aggregating network traffic from every device and application in the data center, including physical and virtual environments, as well as public and private clouds. A distributed layer of high-performance nodes forms a network visibility infrastructure that provides a view of the entire environment to every applicable security or monitoring tool.

Getting RESTful

As you well know, it's not enough to simply look at traffic. You also must respond to suspected or identified threats to prevent their propagation. Ideally, this response is automated, which is where RESTful (representational state transfer) APIs come into play.

A network visibility appliance integrates a set of open, RESTful APIs into the network visibility infrastructure, enabling security and other network monitoring tools to interact directly with the traffic. Security ops folks can leverage these open RESTful APIs in an SDP to develop and use a programmable framework to enhance network visibility. With RESTful APIs, you can automate functions in the infrastructure, such as a dynamic response to detected threats. This automation helps minimize the effect of threats and improves IT's agility in responding to those threats.

Chapter 3

Exploring Features and Use Cases

*N*etwork visibility appliances — which are key components of a security delivery platform (SDP) — offer several advanced features and use cases that address a wide range of network security and monitoring needs. We discuss those features and uses in this chapter.

Advanced Network Visibility Appliance Features

To do their jobs, network security tools need to see the traffic that is of interest to them — nothing more and nothing less. Network visibility appliances are designed to optimize the efficiency and effectiveness of security tools by helping them to do just that. We discuss some of the advanced features of these appliances in the following sections.

Packet filtering

Packet filtering does exactly what the name says: filters packets based on specified criteria before forwarding them to the security tool(s). Packet filtering helps reduce the volume of traffic for security and monitoring tools by extracting desired packets (performed by a positive filter) or dropping unwanted packets (performed by a negative filter).

Both positive and negative filters can filter packets based on specific criteria, such as the following:

- Internet protocol (IP) address (source, destination, range)

- Media access control (MAC) address (source and/or destination)

- Transmission control protocol (TCP), user datagram protocol (UDP), and Internet control message protocol (ICMP) (port, range)

- Virtual local area network (VLAN), quality of service (QoS), and IP service layer

Packet de-duplication

Multiple copies of the same packet can overload security and monitoring tools. De-duplication eliminates copies to improve performance.

When packets are gathered from multiple collection points along a path, the packet de-duplication feature in the network visibility appliance can relieve tool processing resources by forwarding only one copy of each packet.

Packet slicing and masking

Not every part of every packet is of equal interest or relevance to every security tool. Furthermore, not every part of the packet should be visible to every tool for compliance reasons. Even if the security tool needs only information that applies to Layer 2, 3, or 4, it still has to manage the entire packet for every flow it receives — unless a network visibility appliance performs packet slicing.

Packet slicing increases the processing and monitoring throughput of security tools by reducing packet size. Security tools process fewer bytes while maintaining relevant portions of each packet. Packet slicing significantly increases the capacity of forensic recording tools, as it reduces the amount of storage and the processing capability needed to inspect packets.

Packet masking obscures private and sensitive data (such as financial and medical information) in the packet before that data is delivered to a tool. Packet masking enables IT operators to identify and mask credit card numbers and Social Security numbers across user-level transactions, as well as to identify and mask phone numbers exchanged across session initiation protocol (SIP) packets. Thus, packet masking helps IT organizations comply with privacy and regulatory requirements.

Session-aware load balancing

Session-aware load balancing distributes traffic across multiple ports to maximize throughput and prevent overloading any single port. The system applies weighting to the traffic distribution, supporting different tool capacities. The parallel processing enabled by session-aware load balancing allows an administrator to scale monitoring beyond a single monitoring device.

Load balancing can be based on options including hashing, bandwidth, cumulative traffic, packet rate, connections, and round-robin.

When you use load balancing to distribute network traffic across multiple monitoring tools, it's important to ensure that entire sessions are sent to the same tool. The network visibility appliance uses hashing algorithms across Layer 2 through Layer 4 fields to ensure that packets belonging to the same session are sent to the same tool.

Common Use Cases

This section summarizes key use cases for SDPs. We explore these use cases in detail later in this book.

Facilitating active security devices

Active security devices offer an advantage over passive devices because they can actually stop the threats they detect. Unfortunately, they also create a fair share of friction between network operations and security operations.

 In Chapter 4, we explore how an SDP can smooth over this friction by facilitating active bypass for active security devices.

Securing virtual and cloud environments

Often, when virtualization and cloud computing projects stall, the problem is security. IT must achieve the visibility necessary to secure these environments so that it can expand the organization's virtualization and cloud projects with confidence. We explain how in Chapter 5.

Generating session metadata

Session metadata, in the form of NetFlow/IPFIX, can provide valuable insights into traffic. Network operations traditionally uses NetFlow to obtain summarized traffic reports, but security operations can also leverage it to detect malicious traffic traversing the network.

 Find out more in Chapter 6 about using an SDP to generate session metadata to improve security.

Isolating application traffic for inspection

Significant volumes of network traffic may not be of interest to security appliances. Video and voice traffic, for example, may not always need to be monitored and analyzed. Isolating specific traffic streams for targeted inspection can optimize security efficacy by selectively excluding low-risk traffic, such as voice and video, from the overburdened security inspection tools. We explore this topic further in Chapter 7.

Gaining visibility into SSL-encrypted traffic

IT relies on Secure Sockets Layer (SSL) encryption to protect sensitive and confidential information from eavesdroppers as that information traverses the network. SSL also prevents network security and monitoring tools from inspecting this traffic. This situation wouldn't be a problem if IT could always trust encrypted traffic, but that's simply not the case. Threat actors increasingly use SSL encryption to hide malware and bypass security controls, making it all the more vital for IT organizations to inspect this traffic.

To find out how an SDP can provide visibility into SSL-encrypted traffic, see Chapter 8.

Software-defined visibility

Security appliances are only as effective as the traffic they see. Unfortunately, an enterprise network is a dynamic and complex entity, so providing visibility is an ongoing effort, and it must be automated to be truly effective. (The last thing security administrators need is another item on their to-do list, right?) Enter software-defined visibility.

Software-defined visibility (SDV) is a highly programmable, easy-to-automate framework based on pervasive visibility. A web-services framework based on RESTful (representational state transfer) application programming interfaces (APIs) is integrated directly into the security delivery platform (SDP), enabling any device on the network to interact directly with it as needed. APIs exposed through a centralized

policy controller allow external systems to interact with the network visibility appliances in the platform programmatically. In addition, the RESTful APIs support programmability in the SDP itself, ensuring that new blind spots are detected and eliminated as they emerge.

SDV enables security operations to automate multiple functions within the infrastructure, including dynamic response to detected threat patterns, adjustments to traffic mode configurations for active security tools, and IT operations management functions and capabilities.

SDV is a new approach that makes IT and security administrators more agile, and it fulfills the now-crucial requirement to detect and respond to threats quickly and continuously.

Chapter 4

Facilitating Active Security Devices

*P*erimeter defense continues to play an important role in enterprise security. In addition to using firewalls to filter out general riffraff, many IT organizations deploy active security tools as part of a defense-in-depth security strategy in various segments of the infrastructure.

Deploying active security devices presents its own challenges, however. A network visibility appliance with inline bypass capability can help, as we discuss in this chapter.

Key Challenges of Active Security Devices

The nature of an inline security architecture presents challenges. Whereas passive security tools are designed to sit out of band to monitor network traffic, active security tools sit directly in the path of traffic. As a gatekeeper for all traffic coming into and going out of the network, an active security tool receives and then forwards benign packets after inspection.

Also, unlike passive tools, active security tools can act on traffic by allowing, blocking, and sometimes even modifying packets. This arrangement is great for preventing malicious or suspicious traffic from crossing the network but potentially not so great for network reliability and performance. It can cause delays and has been known to interfere with authorized activity. If the active device goes down, so does the network. The need to prevent malicious traffic with active security devices and the need to ensure network availability pits security operations against network operations.

Another challenge is maintenance, which can result in service failures when tools must be taken offline. Thus, maintenance must be performed when the network isn't experiencing heavy use — typically, early mornings, late evenings, or weekends.

Network visibility appliances solve these challenges by facilitating inline bypass for connected security appliances. This chapter shows you how.

How Inline Bypass Works

A network visibility appliance that supports inline bypass can continue to pass uninspected network traffic in the event that its connected security tool suffers a failure of any kind, such as a loss of power.

Rather than connecting directly to the network, each tool connects to one or more network visibility appliances. Each appliance sits inline, and *it* redirects traffic to and from the active tools (see Figure 4-1). Traffic enters the appliance and is immediately routed to its active tool with near-zero latency. After inspection, approved traffic is forwarded back to the appliance and then to the network and its final destination.

Network visibility appliances with inline bypass functionality support bidirectional traffic, enabling active security tools to inspect both ingress and egress traffic.

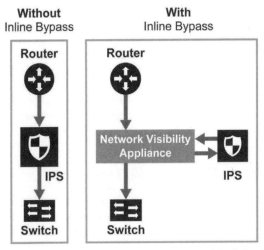

Figure 4-1: A network visibility appliance provides inline bypass protection.

Fault Tolerance

Network visibility appliances that support inline bypass ensure that if an active security tool fails, the network won't go down. This fault tolerance is achieved via the features and capabilities discussed in the following sections.

Failing open or closed

One way to achieve fault tolerance is to implement fail-open policies. *Fail-open policies* ensure that if a security tool fails for any reason (such as a power failure), traffic continues to traverse the network.

For some IT organizations, the cost of network downtime is so high that continued operation is more important than temporary loss of a specific security tool. In such a case, it's better to fail open.

Sometimes, networks are so sensitive that a loss of a specific security tool requires the local area network (LAN) to be disconnected from the public Internet. The network must fail closed. In this case, the network visibility appliance effectively breaks the network connection to prevent traffic from flowing.

Consider the security tool itself when deciding whether to fail open or fail closed. A very real security risk occurs if the network isn't guarded by a firewall, but no one would lose much sleep if a secondary protection device, such as an inline intrusion prevention system (IPS) or data loss prevention (DLP) solution, went offline for a few minutes. Network visibility appliances with bypass capability allow IT organizations to choose the mode that's most appropriate for each security tool.

Link state mirroring

Network redundancy is typically achieved by building redundant communication paths. These paths serve as alternative routes for traffic. If one path goes down, traffic can be routed to another.

For monitoring networks with redundant paths, active tools can be deployed independently or shared between network paths. Network visibility appliances with network link state mirroring capability ensure that downstream or upstream link state can be translated across the inline bypass so that network failover can occur if necessary.

Health-check packets

Given the importance of using an active security tool to prevent attacks and block unauthorized traffic, it's a good idea to verify that the tool is doing its job. You can verify the link state of a tool or check its ability to respond to a network ping. Network visibility appliances, however, offer a better way.

The appliance uses health-check packets to verify a tool's health. *Health-check packets* are bidirectional packets generated by the network visibility appliance and forwarded by the active security tool. If, within a specified interval, the health-check packets don't pass through the security tool, the appliance can take one of four preconfigured actions:

✔ Bypass the security tool and send all traffic directly to the network (fail open).

✔ Disconnect the network connection so that no traffic is allowed through (fail closed).

✔ Forward the traffic to another tool in a load-balanced pool of tools.

✔ Fail over to a standby tool (in a 1+1 or N+1 arrangement).

Health-check packets can detect several types of problems, including a failed connection to the security tool, failure of the tool's hardware or software, or misconfiguration of the tool.

Benefits of Inline Bypass

A network visibility appliance with inline bypass capability introduces a simple change to the network architecture — the addition of the appliance itself — but offers great benefits in deploying active tools. These benefits include the following:

✔ **Maintenance without down time:** Bypass capability makes it easier to maintain security tools without affecting network availability. Because the traffic forwarding state is controllable, network or security operations can configure traffic to bypass the tool that's out of commission. Traffic can be redistributed across remaining tools (see Figure 4-2) or forwarded to a standby tool. When maintenance is complete, IT can reconfigure traffic to pass through.

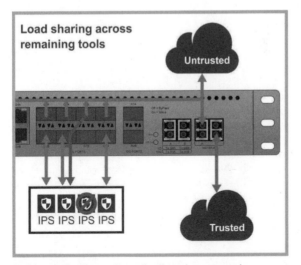

Figure 4-2: Traffic can be redistributed across tools.

✔ **Scaling of active inspection to meet network bandwidth:** Inline bypass enables organizations to distribute traffic across multiple tools of the same type to increase inspection beyond what a single tool can do.

✔ **Fewer after-hours updates:** Connecting active security tools to a network visibility appliance rather than directly to the production network allows IT to seamlessly add, upgrade, or remove tools without affecting network availability. This capability reduces the number of late nights or weekends that IT personnel spend at the office while increasing the department's flexibility and agility.

✔ **Less risk of network outages:** In addition to enabling maintenance outside traditional hours, the pass-through and failover contingencies reduce the risk of network outages. If a security tool shuts down or stops passing traffic, users still have access to the Internet and other network resources, which makes everyone happy.

Chapter 5

Securing Virtual and Cloud Environments

*I*T organizations are increasingly adopting cloud computing and virtualization for agility and scalability benefits. Unfortunately, the elastic, dynamic nature of software-defined cloud computing introduces challenges. IT's ability to respond to business needs is improved, but securing the environment is more difficult. A security delivery platform (SDP) can help, as we discuss in this chapter.

Key Challenges Posed by Cloud and Virtualization

Virtualization creates blind spots within the server infrastructure. Traffic that flows between virtual machines (VMs) on the same physical server never hits the physical network. This problem is particularly acute in blade servers running virtualized workloads and servers with a high VM density. In addition, disaggregation and communication between different application tiers increases the complexity of instrumentation. As a result, IT organizations lose visibility and control of traffic traversing the virtualized server infrastructure.

Virtualization also puts greater demands on monitoring technologies. VMware's vSphere vMotion, for example, enables VMs to migrate from one physical server to another, which allows IT to create a dynamic, automated, and self-optimizing data center with continuous optimization of VMs.

Sounds great, right? This agility adds a new layer of complexity to the server infrastructure. To monitor these environments effectively, administrators need a solution that can be updated seamlessly and automatically to reflect the continuous changes in the infrastructure. Monitoring solutions must also provide monitoring continuity and history.

An additional problem is inter-VM communication. The most common way to provide VM switching connectivity is to use a virtual Ethernet switch, also referred to as a vSwitch. A vSwitch is the software equivalent of a Layer 2 hardware switch, enabling IT to network VMs.

By default, all the VMs on a single host can communicate through the vSwitch. This intra-host traffic doesn't transit the physical network, so it isn't visible to many network security and monitoring tools residing outside the virtual server.

Virtualization vendors attempt to provide visibility via *promiscuous mode,* which allows a monitoring tool connected to the virtual switch to intercept and read every frame passed on to the virtual switch.

Unfortunately, promiscuous mode creates security concerns — and for good reason. Any adapter in promiscuous mode has access to every packet, even those heading to other guests or operating systems.

One option is to use vSphere port-mirroring capability to send all inter-VM traffic to the physical network for inspection. This approach, however, could overload the physical NIC as well as the network with traffic that may not need to be monitored.

A virtual network visibility appliance solves the aforementioned concerns. As IT organizations move more mission-critical workloads to virtual servers, the amount of traffic between VMs residing on the same host also increases. In order to ensure end-to-end service delivery, IT must have visibility into the virtual infrastructure. A virtual network visibility appliance can provide this visibility without introducing security risks. The virtual appliance pushes specific inter-VM traffic flows to external security tools.

How a Virtual Appliance Works

A virtual network visibility appliance provides intelligent filtering. It selects traffic flows between VMs on the same host and sends them to the appropriate network security and monitoring tools (see Figure 5-1).

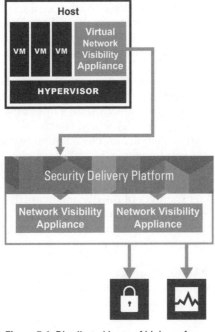

Figure 5-1: Distributed layer of high-performance network visibility appliances forms a network visibility infrastructure.

The virtual network visibility appliance runs as a native VMware vSphere virtual machine, so it doesn't require any agents or changes to the hypervisor. Some older implementations of virtual appliances operate within the hypervisor kernel instead of as native virtual machines. These kernel-based implementations are no longer in vogue, as they require change or validation in response to every hypervisor update. Also, kernel-based implementations can easily and quickly get out of date or crash the hypervisor. A virtual network visibility appliance that operates as a native VM usually continues to operate even if a huge change occurs in the hypervisor software. Administrators get the same packet-level visibility for inter-VM traffic that they get between discrete physical servers.

Traffic flows between VMs on the same host can also be filtered based on user-defined criteria and sent to the appliances on the physical network. The physical appliance collects the traffic and then sends selected traffic to the appropriate network and security tools for inspection.

Virtual network visibility appliances are integrated with virtualization management software such as VMware's vCenter infrastructure and leverage VMware's open application programming interfaces (APIs), which enables them to track agility across high availability and distributed resource scheduler cluster environments. Visibility policies are attached to the monitored VMs. As the VMs migrate across physical hosts in the virtual clusters, the policies move with them. Continuous visibility of the dynamic infrastructure is provided by closed-loop feedback through published APIs to vMotion events and an automation framework that enables visibility policies to synchronize.

Virtual network visibility appliances are also integrated into other environments, such as OpenStack with KVM hypervisor.

Benefits of Virtual Visibility

 Extending the visibility into virtual environments offers several benefits:

✔ **Extended reach:** Shed light on virtualized and cloud environments and thereby extend the reach of monitoring, analytic, and security tools into both intra-host (traffic on the same host) and inter-host (traffic between different hosts) VM traffic. Thus, visibility spans physical, virtual, and software-defined network (SDN) infrastructure across campus, cloud, and carrier environments.

✔ **VM migration:** Unlike physical servers, active VMs may migrate from one host to another. With network visibility, monitoring policies can be automatically migrated to the new host when vMotion occurs. As a result, security tools get continuous visibility into traffic from the virtualized server without any administrative intervention.

✔ **Eliminated host overload:** Often, security administrators place multiple security tools (agents) on the same virtual host. These security tools contend for the same resources as the virtualized workload on that host. Consequently, a limited number of virtual tools can be placed on a single host. The virtual network visibility approach, on the other hand, captures the traffic once and then replicates it to as many security tools as required.

✔ **Consistent view of physical and virtual infrastructure:** By delivering traffic from both the physical and virtual infrastructure, security tools obtain a consistent view of emerging threats from physical, virtual, or even emerging SDN infrastructure.

✔ **Reduced network backhaul:** Network visibility appliances can slice traffic at the source to conserve the amount of traffic that is backhauled from the host — particularly important when the host has network I/O constraints.

Adapting to SDN environments

IT organizations often hit a roadblock on their way to the private cloud: The dynamic virtual world they create is still tied to the physical network. Although an IT admin may be able to provision a VM in a matter of minutes, setting up the necessary network and security services still takes days.

Virtual extensible LAN (VXLAN) helps solve this challenge. VXLAN is a virtual network built on top of Layer 2 and Layer 3 technologies, designed to address scalability problems in cloud computing deployments. VXLAN creates Layer 2 logical networks that are encapsulated in standard Layer 3 IP packets, allowing Layer 2 virtual networks to be extended across physical boundaries. As a result, large numbers of isolated Layer 2 VXLAN networks can live together on a common Layer 3 infrastructure. In addition, VMs can reside on the same Layer 2 virtual network but be on two different Layer 3 networks.

VXLAN isn't perfect. Individual applications flowing within the tunnel can't be monitored, and modifying monitoring tools to do so would force them to spend resource cycles stripping out encapsulations when they should be monitoring traffic. That's where the security delivery platform (SDP) comes in.

VXLAN encapsulated traffic can be sent to the network visibility appliance, which can filter the traffic based on the segment ID to forward and/or decouple traffic before forwarding it to the right monitoring tools. This system gives the network security and monitoring tools the visibility they need to monitor the security and performance of the VXLAN without any hardware or software modifications.

Various SDN implementations have emerged over the past few years, including Cisco's Application Centric Infrastructure (ACI) and VMware's NSX. A well-designed SDP integrates perfectly into such architectures.

Chapter 6

Generating Session Metadata

*A*dvanced persistent threats (APTs) operate low and slow on the network. They move laterally and periodically communicate with command-and-control sites but mostly remain dormant for weeks or even months, so they're nearly impossible to detect without a complete and continuous view of network traffic.

NetFlow is a simple, effective way to increase network visibility that can play a key role in detecting the anomalous traffic patterns that may indicate an APT. The session metadata provided by NetFlow can be used to build relationships and use patterns between network nodes. This contextual information can help augment analysis of network activity to surface APTs. Many security tools, including security information and event management (SIEM) systems, consume NetFlow records to assist in such analysis.

Incorporating NetFlow analysis into your arsenal of cyberse-curity practices has numerous benefits:

✔ Improved ability to detect threats that bypass traditional, signature-based defenses

✔ Improved ability to investigate the causes and effects of network breaches

✔ Reduced storage requirements compared with full-packet-capture security analytics platforms

In this chapter, we explain the challenges of using NetFlow for security analytics and show how you can overcome those challenges to incorporate NetFlow- and metadata-based analysis into your security architecture.

A variation of NetFlow called Internet Protocol Flow Information Export (IPFIX) is used in many deployments. For simplicity, we use *NetFlow* to mean both NetFlow and IPFIX.

Key Challenges of NetFlow Generation

To use NetFlow for security, IT organizations must optimize the architecture that generates and analyzes it. The conventional way of generating NetFlow records presents several challenges:

✔ NetFlow generation can be difficult for routers and switches and can affect their performance. To prevent latency and packet loss, networking devices can be configured to sample packets used for NetFlow record generation rather than sending all packets to the NetFlow generation engine. After sampling, only a percentage of packets are sent to the NetFlow record generation engine. This arrangement reduces the burden on routers and switches but doesn't provide the complete picture required to detect traffic patterns generated by APTs.

✔ Some technology providers have their own versions of NetFlow, which aren't compatible with all security tools.

✔ NetFlow-based data is summarized data. It doesn't provide access to a specific set of packets or packet payloads. Administrators often need full packet payloads to complement NetFlow data in order to do meaningful analysis. Traditional routers and switches can't provide this additional data.

✔ Networking devices such as switches support a limited number of NetFlow collectors. (A NetFlow collector receives, stores, analyzes, and generates reports from the collected flow data.) Contention for those collector ports may limit NetFlow collection and result in partial metadata views in the security tools that need such metadata.

✔ Routers and switches lack the policy-based forwarding capability that would enable IT to generate NetFlow for specific traffic of interest.

IT organizations can address these challenges and gain valuable insight into traffic by offloading NetFlow generation to one or more intelligent network visibility appliances operating within a security delivery platform (SDP).

How NetFlow Generation Works

A network visibility appliance can summarize and generate unsampled NetFlow statistics from incoming traffic streams, thereby offloading this resource-intensive task from networking devices. You can select the traffic flows from which to generate NetFlow statistics and simultaneously send the original packets to the appropriate monitoring tools.

A network visibility appliance that supports NetFlow versions 5 and 9, as well as IPFIX, integrates seamlessly with standards-based collectors. NetFlow records can also be exported to multiple collectors at the same time, providing a single flow source for critical network management applications. In addition, traffic can be filtered so that collectors receive only flow records of interest.

A visibility appliance can expand NetFlow data beyond the information typically summarized in a NetFlow record.

Following are four examples of how NetFlow records can be enriched with such metadata:

- ✓ URL information from HTTP packets can be appended to exported NetFlow records to provide insights into suspicious communication patterns.

- ✓ Session initiation protocol (SIP) information extracted from SIP traffic can provide insights into callers' email addresses.

- ✓ Some HTTP response codes could be used to detect potential server compromise, denial-of-service attacks, and other anomalous traffic patterns.

- ✓ Looking at DNS requests and responses provided as metadata could provide faster insight into suspicious communications.

In addition to providing summarized flow statistics, network visibility appliances can aggregate, replicate, filter, and send raw traffic streams to network security and monitoring tools.

Benefits of Offloading NetFlow Generation

Using a network visibility appliance to generate NetFlow delivers several benefits:

- ✓ The appliance not only relieves networking devices of this resource-intensive task, but also improves the effectiveness of security tools and operations.

- ✓ A network visibility appliance can provide a complete picture of the network by forwarding all packets at line rate and simultaneously generating NetFlow records for selected traffic. Sending this data to security analytics tools makes them much more accurate and effective. Policy-based filtering and forwarding of traffic for NetFlow generation enables IT to specify high-value traffic flows for which NetFlow data is generated and deliver that data to the right security tools at the right time.

✔ Generating accurate NetFlow records from remote locations instead of backhauling entire traffic streams to a central site can reduce bandwidth consumption. Centralizing NetFlow collection can reduce the number of collectors needed as well as bandwidth consumed — particularly helpful for monitoring remote sites and branch offices connected via low-bandwidth connections.

✔ NetFlow is a cost-effective way to analyze areas of the network that aren't being monitored. It can be used to analyze vast amounts of internal traffic. If the NetFlow collector sees any suspicious activity or NetFlow flags something suspicious, it can request that the SDP forward the entire packet stream to centralized security tools for more in-depth analysis. Thus, IT can achieve security in depth without deploying deep packet inspection on every network segment, which would increase cost.

✔ Centralizing NetFlow generation enables IT organizations to generate flow records for traffic flows that could be seen anywhere by the SDP. This approach prevents a sprawl of NetFlow appliances.

✔ Accurate NetFlow records with rich contextual metadata can assist in the detection of APTs. NetFlow analytics tools look for odd or anomalous traffic patterns on the network, such as frequency and source of DNS queries or traffic on unique port/protocol combinations. Because NetFlow information can be parsed for bandwidth consumption, application type, and source, it allows analytics tools to hone in on malicious activity faster and potentially reduce time to discovery.

You can get even more out of NetFlow data by correlating it with data from other tools. Security operations can identify the users and/or devices associated with suspicious network traffic by correlating media access control (MAC) and IP addresses from NetFlow with threat information from intrusion prevention systems and logon information from lightweight directory access protocol (LDAP) stores.

Additional NetFlow collector database queries can uncover all IP connections made from the compromised device, enabling IT to determine which connections are legitimate and which may be botnet communications. As in the detection of APTs, using NetFlow to detect compromised devices can result in faster analytics processing, as well as faster discovery and remediation.

Chapter 7

Isolating Application Traffic for Targeted Inspection

· ·

In This Chapter

▶ Reviewing the limitations of traditional application filtering

▶ Understanding application session filtering

▶ Recognizing the benefits of application session filtering

· ·

*T*hanks in large part to streaming video, the volume of network traffic is skyrocketing. Network security and monitoring tools must search all this network traffic for signatures of known threats — a task that's getting increasingly difficult.

In this chapter, we explain how application session filtering can facilitate traffic inspection.

Key Challenges with Traditional Traffic Filtering

The growing volume and variety of traffic traversing enterprise networks pose quite a challenge to network security and monitoring tools. It's not necessary for every tool to inspect every single packet, yet that's what often happens. As a result, security tools waste valuable computing resources inspecting enormous volumes of irrelevant traffic.

Simply filtering and sending individual packets to security tools doesn't do the job. Security tools must see the entire traffic session, from initiation to termination, to identify and analyze threats effectively. Without this visibility, security tools generate errors, and some traffic goes uninspected.

In addition, filtering has to go beyond the port number. At one point, it made sense to match applications based on destination port and protocol. If traffic was headed to transmission control protocol (TCP) port 80, for example, a firewall would know that the traffic stream required security inspection.

Today, however, hundreds of applications can run over the same TCP/user datagram protocol (UDP) port. To determine how to handle traffic properly, network security or monitoring devices need more detailed information about each application.

Further, incident response teams look for specific patterns within certain applications to identify occurrence of incidents, narrow down infected endpoints, and perform necessary cleanup. (A popular worm and its variants used sequences of repeating characters in HTTP packets to exploit insecure web servers, for example.) Searching for infected machines involves looking for suspicious patterns in your network traffic to identify the source and destination of these flows.

A network visibility appliance addresses these problems by pulling out specific traffic flows that belong to an application or a pattern of interest and then sending them to the appropriate security tools.

How Application Session Filtering Works

A filtering engine in the network visibility appliance identifies applications based on signatures or patterns that can appear across any part of the packet payload. These patterns can be as simple as a static string at a user-configured offset or as complex as an extremely advanced Perl Compatible Regular Expression (PCRE) at a variable offset.

A session can be any of the following:

- ✔ TCP session
- ✔ UDP session
- ✔ Subset of fields in a standard IP 5-tuple (IPv4/v6 source address, IPv4/v6 destination address, source port, destination port, and protocol)

A network visibility appliance's application session filtering function is distinct from advanced packet filtering. Although advanced packet filtering can identify matching content in packets, application session filtering goes a step further by identifying entire traffic sessions that belong to a specific application. After identification, the entire traffic session can be filtered out. This system is valuable when a specific type of application session (such as Netflix traffic) need not be sent to the security tool. Alternatively, only traffic for that specific session of interest (such as a new web application) can be sent to the security tool. Some vendors provide scripts for popular applications, which makes implementing application session filtering faster and easier.

Benefits of Application Session Filtering

Application session filtering has several benefits:

- ✔ **Tool optimization:** The most notable benefit of application session filtering is that it enables IT organizations to optimize network security and monitoring tools for traffic inspection. Forwarding only relevant traffic corresponding to an *entire* session to these tools increases their efficacy, and reducing the volume of traffic that they receive vastly improves their performance. As a result, tools can process traffic faster, and IT organizations can reduce the time it takes to detect threats on the network.

- ✔ **Identification of legitimate traffic:** Along the same lines, IT organizations can manage non-work-related application traffic (such as streaming video) to prevent this low-value, low-risk traffic from overwhelming security tools.

- ✔ **Identification of legitimate applications:** Application session filtering enables IT to identify applications based on one or more combinations of packet content, ports, URLs, and HTTP content. It can also provide visibility into traffic transmitted over HTTP to ensure that the traffic is coming from legitimate applications.

✔ **Use of custom regular expressions:** IT organizations can use custom regular expressions to detect traffic patterns associated with risky applications or malicious communications and then direct that traffic to security tools for further analysis or blocking. This arrangement minimizes the organization's risk exposure and liability.

Network traffic makes the grade at GWU

Streaming services such as Netflix and Hulu represents a whopping 50 percent of George Washington University's network traffic. Given that this data doesn't require the same level of scrutiny as other traffic traversing the network, the university's IT team was concerned that its passive security sensors were being overwhelmed with traffic that didn't need inspection. To complicate matters, the university runs multiple data centers. So the team turned to Gigamon for a solution.

Gigamon previously helped the university deploy its GigaSMART® deduplication technology to reduce the number of duplicate packets passing through its security tools. Gigamon also helped the university feed multiple connections into a consolidated set of security tools to increase visibility across the network.

To improve security tool performance, Gigamon recommended that the university leverage the application session filtering capability within its GigaSMART platform. This solution enabled the university to identify Netflix and Hulu traffic in the payload and to eliminate entire traffic sessions associated with them, ensuring that security tools received only relevant traffic.

The university significantly reduced the video streaming traffic on its network. The application generating this traffic previously was one of the top five applications routing data through the university's security and application performance tools. After GigaSMART was deployed, the application dropped to one of the top 25.

The university also took advantage of centralized security processing and scaled this protection across multiple data centers. Threat detection coverage expanded across the security infrastructure, including an intrusion prevention system, a network threat prevention platform, advanced persistent threat and malware protection tools, and a forensic packet capture tool.

Chapter 8

Gaining Visibility into SSL-Encrypted Traffic

In This Chapter

▶ Identifying the key challenges of SSL-encrypted data

▶ Decrypting SSL traffic

▶ Offloading SSL decryption to a network visibility appliance

*O*ver the years, IT organizations have come to depend on Secure Sockets Layer (SSL) technology for encrypting and authenticating data online. SSL plays an important role in keeping a wide range of web services secure, including email, e-commerce, Voice over IP (VoIP) communications, and online banking. SSL has also become a vital technology for delivering secure cloud-based services. The very technology that keeps private data safe from peering eyes, however, makes it more difficult for IT organizations to secure their networks. In this chapter, you look at how IT organizations can efficiently decrypt SSL traffic to achieve crucial visibility.

Transport Layer Security (TLS) is a successor to SSL. In this chapter, we use *SSL* to mean both TLS and SSL.

Challenges of Decrypting SSL Traffic

IT's network visibility challenges are exacerbated by the increasing use of SSL encryption, which can mask sensitive or private data as well as malicious content. As a result, cybercriminals increasingly use SSL encryption to hide botnets and other malware.

The challenge lies in IT's ability to decrypt SSL traffic. Most passive security and monitoring tools can't decrypt or monitor this growing segment of traffic. Some active security tools integrate SSL decryption, but enabling this feature decreases device performance by as much as 80 percent.

Hardware upgrades are often necessary to facilitate SSL decryption. The computing load increases as organizations use more cloud-based services and certificate authorities implement longer keys (such as 256-bit SSL encryption based on a 2,048-bit key).

IT organizations also have to deal with the privacy implications of decrypting SSL traffic. Many organizations are required to meet strict regulatory requirements and industry standards to protect data privacy. Controls must be in place to prevent decrypted data from being misused and to ensure that sensitive data remains secure. Without these controls, IT organizations open themselves to costly regulatory compliance violations.

IT organizations must acquire visibility into SSL sessions so that network security and analytics tools can monitor encrypted traffic for potential threats. SSL decryption functionality in a network visibility appliance can do just that.

How SSL Decryption Works

A network visibility appliance with integrated SSL support can provide insight into network traffic blind spots. SSL sessions are quickly decrypted to uncover hidden security threats. When packets are decrypted, they're sent from the production network to multiple out-of-band tools for monitoring and analysis.

Decrypting SSL traffic with a network visibility appliance is a five-step process (see Figure 8-1):

1. **Install the visibility appliance with SSL decryption capability.**

2. **Select the traffic flows to monitor.**

   The visibility appliance identifies the exchange of public keys at the beginning of the transaction.

3. The administrator uploads the private keys, which are encrypted and securely stored.

4. Using the private and public keys, the visibility appliance decrypts SSL traffic.

5. The visibility appliance sends decrypted packets to monitoring tools or applies additional operations to the traffic.

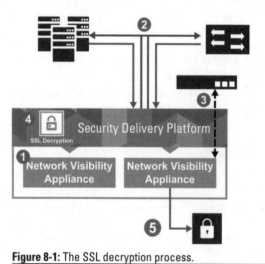

Figure 8-1: The SSL decryption process.

After SSL traffic is decrypted, other traffic intelligence operations can be applied by the network visibility appliance to modify, manipulate, transform, and deliver traffic to the connected management, monitoring, and security tools. By combining these applications and applying them to different traffic types, IT organizations can maximize security. SSL traffic can be decrypted and then masked, for example, so that regulated data (such as financial or medical data) can be hidden in compliance with regulatory requirements.

In a nutshell, the IT organization should have access to the private keys of the servers, as they need to be loaded into the visibility appliance to facilitate decryption of the flows.

Benefits of SSL Decryption

SSL decryption provides numerous benefits:

✓ **Increased efficiency:** Offloading SSL decryption to a network visibility appliance in a security delivery platform (SDP) optimizes security. It frees security tool resources for packet analysis, thereby improving their performance. Decryption is performed once, and the decrypted traffic is sent to multiple tools. This delivers immediate value and return on investment as IT organizations reduce their capital expenditure, licensing fees, and management costs.

✓ **Improved scalability:** Any traffic received on any network port of the SDP can be decrypted and sent to any tool attached to the SDP — an important feature, because not every tool attached to an SDP requires SSL decryption capability.

✓ **Efficient use of resources:** Organizations no longer have to install SSL decryption tools throughout the network infrastructure to access encrypted traffic. Centralizing tools and offering SSL decryption through the SDP reduces costs and improves efficiency so that fewer but more capable tools can be used to better effect. The SDP extends SSL decryption capability throughout the visibility infrastructure, so SSL decryption can be selectively applied to any traffic that enters the visibility infrastructure. SSL decryption offered by the SDP can be easily scaled, allowing inspection to grow in response to growing SSL processing needs.

✓ **Improved visibility:** Finally, a network visibility appliance delivers the visibility and control that IT needs to make better, more informed security decisions while meeting regulatory compliance requirements. Visibility into encrypted traffic supports malware detection, intrusion detection, data-loss prevention, and network forensics. It also allows the IT organization to monitor cloud-based traffic and to build trusted cloud services and SSL connections.

Chapter 9

Getting Started with a Security Delivery Platform

In This Chapter

▶ Setting up a security delivery platform (SDP)

▶ Extending an SDP to nonsecurity tools for maximum value

*S*etting up a security delivery platform (SDP) is a straight-forward process. In this chapter, you dive into a six-step process to help you get started with an SDP and begin realizing the benefits of a visibility-focused approach to security.

Step 1: TAP All Critical Links

Visibility across all critical assets and traffic is essential. The best way to ensure overall visibility is to adopt a "TAP-all" strategy.

In other words, all links that carry important information from user to server, user to Internet, or server to server should be connected to a test access point (TAP). Critical links may include those to your DHCP, DNS, Active Directory, database, and web servers; application delivery controllers; firewalls; and WAN routers.

 Don't forget your remote sites and virtualized infrastructures. Too often, security personnel have little to zero visibility into their virtual and cloud environments. Put TAPs everywhere — including virtual TAPs that can monitor traffic flowing to, from, and between your virtual servers.

If you're considering deploying active security tools, be sure to use bypass TAPs (see Chapter 4).

Step 2: Connect TAPs to a High-Availability SDP

After you install TAPs on all critical links, you connect them to an SDP, from which you can build multi-tiered security.

With an SDP, you can aggregate, filter, replicate, and intelligently modify traffic to your security tools. These functions not only optimize security tool performance and eliminate blind spots but also enhance the efficiency and performance of all your applications.

Step 3: Connect Active Security Tools to the SDP

The third step in the process involves distributing traffic to inline defense-in-depth stacks.

Chances are that you're using multiple active security tools, such as next-generation firewalls (NGFWs), advanced intrusion prevention systems (IPSes), and web application firewalls. Whenever you need to upgrade, add, or delete tools, you have to coordinate with your network team to find a mutually acceptable maintenance window. With an SDP, however, you can begin to operationalize this process and perform these operations independently without any effect on the network.

Rather than create the lowest common denominator across your entire stack of security tools, you can use the bypass function in an SDP. This approach has several benefits:

✔ With bypass, you can pick and choose specific traffic of interest to distribute across your various active security tools while bypassing the rest of the traffic.

✔ If an active security tool fails, the failure won't affect the entire network, as the SDP can be configured to bypass the failed tool. This approach maximizes resiliency and security efficacy while simplifying operations.

> ✔ Because any inline deployment represents a potential
> point of failure or bottleneck, bypass can mitigate those
> risks as explained in Chapter 4.

See Chapter 4 for details on setting up inline bypass.

Step 4: Connect Passive Security Tools to the SDP

The next step is taking inventory of your passive security
devices and connecting them to the SDP.

Do you have email inspection gateways, data loss prevention
(DLP) appliances, intrusion detection systems (IDSes), or
packet capture devices, all of which need to inspect traffic out
of band? What about security information and event management (SIEM) and forensics tools? These are all great candidates
to connect directly to an SDP.

When all relevant devices are connected, an SDP can ensure
that the right traffic is sent to the right security tools at the
right time. It can specify that a security tool that specializes in
monitoring emails for threats isn't fed any nonmail traffic, for
example, while ensuring that mail isn't sent to tools designed
for web applications or database monitoring.

In addition to achieving full security visibility and improving
threat detection accuracy, you maximize the performance of
all security tools connected to the SDP.

Step 5: Leverage Traffic Intelligence

How much traffic is too much? If your security tools can't
cope with the amount of traffic they're receiving, you may
have too much. Or perhaps you could benefit from intelligent
forwarding and filtering to reduce unnecessary traffic.

You can reduce traffic in multiple ways, including

✓ **Isolate flows of interest.** To maximize the efficiency of security tools, you can select specific flows of interest for a security tool. You could apply a filter that shows only traffic coming from outside the organization, for example — nothing from inside. Or you could choose to look at specific sessions of interest rather than all traffic.

✓ **Prune voluminous traffic.** Because external traffic can be voluminous, you may benefit from filtering out uninteresting items. You could choose to filter out YouTube or Netflix traffic, for example, partly because it's voluminous and partly because it's not a point of attack. You don't need to send this type of traffic to IDSes or any other advanced threat defense appliances. Refer to Chapter 7 for details on application session filtering.

✓ **Leverage metadata.** If you'd like to have the option to extract metadata, consider using something like NetFlow/IPFIX (Internet Protocol Flow Information Export) generation to maximize effectiveness. Or if you want to see what URLs have been accessed or get a better understanding of who contacted whom, at what time, and for how long, you can leverage an SDP's metadata-generation capabilities.

Step 6: Add Nonsecurity Tools to Maximize Value

An SDP can also provide the same scaling and traffic intelligence benefits to your nonsecurity tools, such as those that you use for application and network performance, user experience, and business services monitoring. You can add any of these types of tools to expand your visibility across the network, into the cloud, and within encrypted sessions and encapsulated packets — all without affecting security monitoring or leaving the network vulnerable. So why not connect them, too, alongside your security devices and further maximize the value of your SDP and the tools themselves?

Chapter 10

Ten Buying Criteria for Security Delivery Platforms

A security delivery platform (SDP) can transform the way that IT organizations secure their networks. An SDP gives complete visibility across extended data center, campus, and branch networks, and offloads many computationally intensive processes from network security and monitoring tools. IT organizations get a more effective security architecture that's optimized for surfacing threats with the smallest possible footprint.

This chapter gives you ten criteria for selecting an SDP.

Broad Selection of Models

The enterprise network is anything but static, and sooner or later, the increasing volume of traffic will drive network upgrades.

IT organizations should choose an SDP from a provider that offers a broad selection of network visibility appliances, including both physical and virtual versions. A futureproof SDP can scale and grow with network speeds and traffic loads.

Network visibility appliances enable you to select the media modules that suit your needs — copper or fiber, 100 Mbps to 100 Gbps and beyond. The appliances should be modular so that adjusting the available port type and densities, as well as upgrading to new and different technologies, is a simple process, ensuring that the SDP meets current and future needs.

Centralized Management and Administration

Pervasive visibility into network blind spots requires the coordination of many components and capabilities. Unless these functional areas and the associated hardware are centrally managed, an SDP offers limited return on investment.

Look for an SDP that provides centralized management, monitoring, and configuration of the physical and virtual traffic policies for a unified approach. The centralized management console should allow managers to map and direct network traffic to the tools and analytics infrastructure.

Support for Virtual and Cloud Environments

Virtualization and cloud technologies are here to stay, and their footprints are growing. The most advanced IT organizations increasingly use them for mission-critical workloads.

To benefit fully from the agility afforded by virtualization and cloud computing, however, IT organizations must address related security concerns. Choose an SDP that enables you to extend visibility into the virtualized servers/cloud infrastructure. Pay particular attention to compatibility with your virtualization stack.

Application Session Filtering

Network security and monitoring tools are bombarded by a growing volume and variety of traffic, and they're becoming overtaxed. IT organizations have two options for keeping up with the increasing flow of traffic:

- ✔ Deploy additional security tools, and increase capital and operating expenditures as a result.
- ✔ Dedicate finite security tool processing cycles to high-value functions. Peel off high-risk traffic for analysis instead of trying to analyze increasing volumes of low-value traffic such as streaming media.

An SDP can generate immediate return on investment by filtering application traffic for specific tools. As a result, existing network security and monitoring tools perform more efficiently because they save CPU cycles otherwise spent filtering out unwanted traffic, allowing IT to do more with existing computing resources.

Flow Metadata Generation

IT organizations need all the help they can get in detecting advanced persistent threats. As we explain in Chapter 6, NetFlow offers valuable insights into traffic that can be used for this purpose. Simply analyzing the NetFlow generated by routers and switches isn't enough. To use NetFlow for security purposes, IT organizations need to offload its generation and analysis to an SDP that can generate unsampled NetFlow records. Then the security tools can obtain as complete a record of traffic as possible.

SSL Traffic Visibility

An SDP provides pervasive visibility of network traffic on behalf of security devices that need it to uncover malicious traffic and threats. With SSL-encrypted traffic becoming an emerging threat source, the SDP that your IT organization chooses should provide SSL traffic visibility via decryption.

Offloading this functionality from your network security and monitoring tools to an SDP not only improves their performance, but also delivers better protection.

APIs for Advanced Integration

To get a leg up on network threats, IT organizations must automate threat response. For this reason, IT organizations should select an SDP that supports application programming interfaces (APIs) for advanced integration of security tools with the SDP.

RESTful (representational state transfer) API support enables advanced integration with tools, controllers, and other IT systems to enable rapid programmatic response to detected events. In other words, you can respond to threats in real time, thereby reducing the time to containment and the risk of data exfiltration.

Enterprise-Class Scalability

With the pervasive visibility afforded by an SDP, IT organizations have the confidence to expand their adoption of virtualization and cloud computing services. The SDP you choose should be scalable to maintain that visibility.

Look for an SDP that provides flexible architecture, with any-to-any port connectivity at line speed for 100 Mbps to 100 Gbps, as well as early support for emerging technologies. It should also support a common management console for large deployments of network visibility appliances and offer custom traffic selection support with parameters for defining traffic forwarding policy. Finally, it should be tool- and network-agnostic so that it can deliver full visibility in heterogeneous environments.

Ease of Use, Speed of Deployment

The last thing IT needs is another application or architecture that's difficult to deploy and use. An SDP should not only optimize security, but also be easy to use and quick to deploy so that IT realizes value from the investment quickly and can rapidly improve the organization's security posture.

Superior Customer Support

High-quality customer support is an important criterion for selecting any vendor, especially an SDP provider.

Select a vendor that offers a broad range of service and support solutions to help you confidently deploy and maintain your SDP. As you implement new technologies and architecture, the provider's professional services team should be available to help you maintain high availability, solve problems quickly, and grow your SDP to meet business needs.

Glossary

● ●

active: A category of security tools that can allow, drop, or modify packets. Active security tools sit inline. See also *inline.*

advanced persistent threat (APT): A sophisticated, targeted cyberattack that employs advanced stealth techniques to bypass traditional signature-based security tools and remain undetected for extended periods.

appliance sprawl: The proliferation of appliances that occurs when IT organizations deploy duplicate security appliances across the network to achieve complete network visibility.

application programming interface (API): A set of programming instructions that specifies how software components should interact.

application session filtering: A capability that allows a network visibility appliance to identify traffic flows belonging to specific application sessions and either send packets of the entire session to the appropriate security tool or drop them.

bring your own device (BYOD): A corporate program or policy that allows employees to use personally owned computing devices to access network resources and conduct business.

bypass TAP (test access point): A simple hardware device that connects directly between two network devices, such as a switch and router, forwards network traffic to an inline security tool, receives (approved) traffic back from that tool, and forwards the inspected traffic to its intended destination.

consumerization of IT: The emergence of technology in consumer markets and the widespread use of that technology in business and government. See also *BYOD.*

daisy chain: A network topology in which nodes or devices are connected as a series and traffic flows through them in a linear sequence.

fail closed: A feature of a network security or monitoring appliance that prevents traffic from passing through if a loss of power or software failure prevents traffic from being inspected.

fail open: A feature of a network security or monitoring appliance that allows traffic to continue to pass uninspected should a loss of appliance power or software failure occur.

health-check packets: Packets that are introduced into the traffic stream by a network visibility appliance and forwarded by a security tool to verify that the tool is operating properly. If the packet doesn't make it through the tool within a given period, there's a problem with the tool.

hub and spoke: A network topology in which one network security or monitoring device serves as a hub and provides a connection point and transit path for other nodes or devices in the same interconnected architecture.

inline: A deployment mode for security tools that puts the tool in the direct path of network traffic. Inline tools can block, allow, or even modify packets as they cross the monitored link. Examples of inline security tools include intrusion prevention systems, next-generation firewalls, and data loss prevention systems.

inline bypass: A capability within a network visibility appliance that serves as a fail-safe for inline security tools. If an inline security tool fails, the network goes down with it. Using inline bypass capability, a network visibility appliance can redirect traffic to secondary routes to maintain production network availability, or to secondary tools to maintain security.

NetFlow: Network session metadata that can be used to analyze traffic for anomalous behavior. NetFlow generation is typically performed by network routers and switches but can be offloaded to a network visibility appliance. NetFlow may be used generically to refer to a family of flow protocols, including IPFIX and sFlow, though the protocols often have fundamental differences.

network TAP (test access point): A simple hardware device that connects directly between two network devices, such as a switch and router, and makes a copy of passing traffic for inspection by out-of-band security tools.

network visibility appliance: A sophisticated network device designed to help network security and performance tools run more efficiently by feeding them and acting on traffic streams that they may not see otherwise.

out of band: In the context of security tools, a mode of operation in which the security tool analyzes copied traffic rather than actual traffic flowing on the network. Unlike an active security tool that sits inline, a security tool that sits out of band can't block or alter traffic; rather, it reports on observed activity and may send actionable alerts based on the observed behavior.

oversubscription: An event in which the available processing power or packet forwarding ability is exceeded. When tool oversubscription occurs, the tool may forward uninspected packets (inline), drop packets (inline), or overwrite older queued packets with newer packets before they can be inspected (out of band). When network oversubscription occurs, packets are dropped.

packet de-duplication: A capability that allows a network visibility appliance to examine and eliminate duplicate packets from a selected traffic stream before they're sent to a security tool for inspection.

packet filtering: A capability that allows a network visibility appliance to identify traffic based on specified criteria and then forward that traffic to security tools for inspection or drop it.

packet masking: A capability that allows a network visibility appliance to obscure private or sensitive data in a packet before it's forwarded to security tools.

packet slicing: A capability that allows a network visibility appliance to truncate selected packets before forwarding them to security tools for analysis.

passive: A category of tools that monitors a copy of packets in the network without the ability to drop/modify the traffic in the production network.

regular expression: A programming string variable or equation that describes a search pattern. Regular expressions can be used with a network visibility appliance to detect traffic associated with risky applications or malicious communications.

Secure Sockets Layer (SSL): A standard security technology that creates an encrypted link between a web server and a client device. SSL protects the data transmitted through this link by rendering it illegible to eavesdroppers. SSL can just as easily be used to transmit malicious data. SSL is generically used to refer to a family of old and new encryption technologies and usually isn't intended to be a literal reference to the original protocol.

security delivery platform (SDP): A structured, platform-based approach to providing traffic visibility to a variety of security appliances in a scalable, pervasive, and cost-effective manner.

software-defined visibility (SDV): A programmable, easy-to-automate framework that uses software to provide visibility across the network.

SPAN port: A switch port used to send a copy of selected traffic for out-of-band monitoring and security use. SPAN ports (or mirror ports) may be configured to duplicate traffic from a variety of sources, including a single port, a group of ports, or one or more VLANs.

SPAN-port contention: A situation that results when an organization has more out-of-band security tools than network access points. This problem is a common one, because most network switches support only a limited number of SPAN output ports, and many tools need to see traffic that's available only from those ports.

time stamping: A capability that allows a network visibility appliance to append a permanent arrival time record to packets at line rate. Time stamping is used to verify packet order and timing for network troubleshooting and analysis.

virtual network visibility appliance: A virtualized network visibility appliance that exposes traffic associated with virtualized workloads and forwards that traffic to security tools.

Notes

Notes